To My Earthly
Angel Amma —
I appreciate You for
and Wonderful Being
I Love You Forever In A
Love
Day!

Pop Pop

# LAKEESHA WALROND

Malachite Unlimited, Inc.
P.O. Box 550
New York, NY 10026

Manufactured in the United States
Second  Edition 2017

Library of Congress Catalog Card Number 1-5760467971

To my mother Deborah - who taught me courage.

**My Body is Special** is the first book of the 'Let's Talk About It' series. This book is inspired by my own story of survival.  Unfortunately, my story is not unique - as there are millions of adult men and women who endured molestation and abuse during their childhood. Often, conversations about abuse do not happen until the abuse is reported. This series encourages adults to have healthy conversations with children about this sensitive topic in an effort to minimize the advantage of those who prey on the innocence of children, and prevent sexual abuse from happening. The conversation between Eva and her mother is one that I hope all parents will have with their children.

This book is intended to be read one-on-one or in a small group setting. The subject matter is very sensitive and may not function as well in large group discussions. There is also an accompanying workbook that helps children develop an individual plan of prevention by identifying what to do, what to say, where to go and who to tell if they ever feel unsafe around another person.

For further information about this topic please refer to your local, state, or national child abuse center.

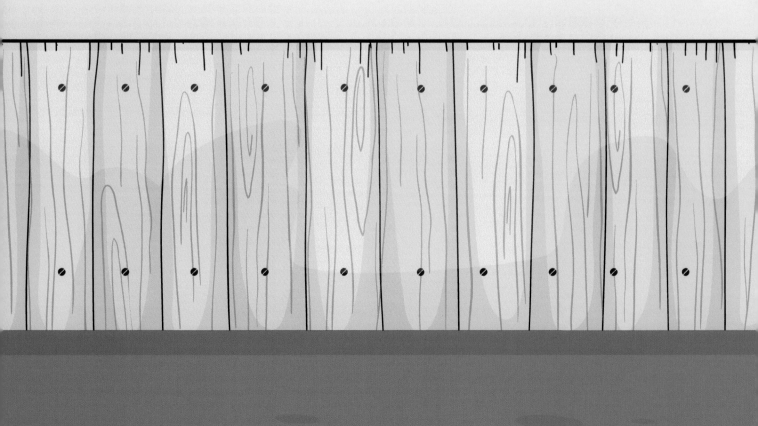

# My Body is Special

Created & Written by LaKeesha Walrond, Ph.D.

Illustrated by Dominiqué Williams-Blair & Phillip Sidberry

Creative Direction by Aaron Brown & Artoholiks

My name is Eva.
I am six years old.

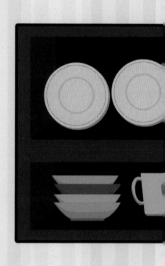

1

My mommy told me something that I want to tell you.

2

She said my body is very special.
It is a true gift.

She said that it is the only body I will get.
I have to take good care of my body.

4

My mommy said I have special places on my body. My special places are those I cover when I wear a two piece swim suit.

Those places are what make girls and boys different from each other.

My mommy told me that no one should ever touch me in my special places.

Then she told me that no one should ever ask me to touch them in their special places.

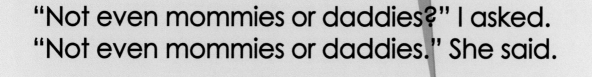

"Not even mommies or daddies?" I asked.
"Not even mommies or daddies." She said.

9

"Not even aunts or uncles?" I asked.
"Not even aunts or uncles." She said.

"Not even people at school or people at church?
I asked.

"Not even people at school or people at church."
She said.

12

"Nobody?" I asked
"Nobody." She said.

I asked my mommy, "What should I do if someone tries to touch me in my special places?"

15

My mommy said that I should say,
"No! Stop! You can not touch me there!"

Then I should scream it again, run away and tell
someone.

I asked my mommy, "What should I do if someone asks me to touch them in their special places?"

My mommy said that I should say, "No! Stop! I can not touch you there!"

Then I should scream it again, run away and tell someone.

I can tell my mommy or daddy.

I can tell another family member.

20

I can tell my school counselor or teacher.

I can tell any adult that I trust.

I hope no one ever tries to touch me in my special places.

If they do, I am glad that I know what I will say.
I will say, "No! Stop! You can not touch me there!"

23

What will you say if it happens to you?

If that ever happens to me I know what I will do.
I will run and scream.

What will you do if it happens to you?

If that ever happens to me I know where I will go.
I will go home or to the nearest safe place I know.

Where will you go if it happens to you?

26

If that ever happens to me I know who I will tell.
I will tell my mommy.

If she is not home, I will tell my Aunt Rose.

27

Who will you tell if it happens to you?

I hope that never happens to me.
I hope that never happens to you.

I am glad that I know what to do if it does happen. I bet you are glad too!

# SAY + DO + GO + TELL

| | |
|---|---|
| **SAY** | No and stop |
| **DO** | Run and scream |
| **GO** | To a safe place |
| **TELL** | Any adult I trust |